by Peter Deneff

ISBN 978-0-7935-9590-7

HAL•LEONARD®
CORPORATION

7777 W. BLUEMOUND RD. P.O. BOX 13819 MILWAUKEE, WI 53213

Visit Hal Leonard Online at
www.halleonard.com

About the Author

Peter Deneff is a pianist, composer, arranger, and teacher at Musicians Institute in Hollywood, California. He began playing piano at age three and started his formal training at age nine. His teachers have included classical pianist Leaine Gibson and jazz pianist Mike Garson.

Peter is currently recording his new CD, *Excursion*, a spicy mixture of Latin jazz and Middle Eastern styles, and is also performing, arranging, and doing studio work in the Los Angeles area.

Introduction

The guitar is perhaps one of the most stylistically versatile instruments in existence. It can be found in all parts of the world and has been adopted into most kinds of music. I have heard guitarists who are well-versed in jazz, blues, and the many incarnations of rock and pop styles. I have also witnessed some incredible technical feats in more unlikely genres such as Arabic, Greek, Armenian, Persian, African and other world styles. Of course, one shouldn't forget the acoustic styles like bluegrass, flamenco, Brazilian, Salsa, and Western European art music (classical). However, one thing I have found about instrumentalists in general, guitarists included, is that we tend to stick with melodic lines that are comfortable to play on our specific instruments. Every instrument has its strengths and weaknesses, and the guitar is no exception. Being a pianist and composer, I often compose parts for the guitar with little or no regard for how they are going to be executed on the instrument. Because of composers' general apathy towards instrumentalists' weaknesses, many musicians find themselves sweating bullets in the middle of a recording session or rehearsal. This is the motivation behind the exercises I composed for *Guitar Hanon*.

This book is intended as a sort of guitar sequel to Charles Louis Hanon's *The Virtuoso Pianist in Sixty Exercises*, a classic of piano literature that has been pushing pianists' technique to the limit for over one hundred years. Much like Hanon's original opus, the exercises in this book are quite playable on the guitar but do not lay out very naturally on the instrument. Many of them are actually taken from pieces I have composed or lines I like to play when I improvise. Once this book has been mastered, you will have dramatically increased strength and independence of your fingering hand and greatly improved speed and coordination of your picking hand.

Because of the many positions one can play on the guitar, I have offered different fingerings for many of the exercises. They can be played on different string sets, in different positions, or across the whole fretboard. I feel it is important to be able to comfortably play through both the latitude and the longitude of the fretboard. There are many positional options on the fretboard, and they should be taken advantage of to their fullest extent. Once you have mastered the given fingerings for each exercise, challenge yourself by playing them in other areas of the fretboard.

The exercises in this book are perfect for either the beginner or the professional and can benefit guitarists of all musical genres. They may be practiced as quickly as they can be played cleanly and accurately. Some tips that should be kept in mind when practicing these exercises include the following:

- Start very slowly and deliberately.
- Let all the notes ring out; place your fingering hand accurately within the frets; keep your picking hand synchronized with your fingering hand.
- Keep your fingering hand up on the fingertips with your fingers nicely curved.
- Keep your picking hand relaxed, and keep your tone fat and even. (Tone starts from the fingers and pick, not the guitar or amp!)
- Use a metronome. The metronome will help you develop your sense of time.
- When you master an exercise at a given speed, increase the tempo by one notch on your metronome.
- Relax your body, don't tense up.
- Push yourself—but stop, relax, and stretch if it hurts!

The main thing to remember is to have fun with these exercises, be creative, and find new ways to incorporate these techniques into your music. Last but not least, do not get discouraged. Technique doesn't happen overnight; it may take weeks or even months to master some of these exercises. It will certainly take longer to master them in several positions. Pace yourself, and you will succeed in mastering this book and be well on your way to becoming the next great guitar wizard!

Happy picking,
Peter Deneff

1

♩. = 60-132
II or III

1.	2	1	0	4	2	1	4	2	1	4	3	1	4	3	1	4	2	1	4	2	1	4	3	1
2.	2	1	4	2	1	4	2	1	4	2	1	4	2	1	4	2	1	4	3	1	4	2	1	4
3.	1	4	2	1	4	3	1	4	3	1	4	2	1	4	2	1	4	3	1	4	2	1	4	2
4.	2	1	4	4	2	1	1	4	3	2	1	4	4	3	2	1	4	4	3	2	1	4	4	2

play 4 times

1	3	4	1	2	4	1	2	4	1	3	4	1	3	4	1	2	4	1	2	4	0	1	2
4	1	2	4	1	3	4	1	2	4	1	2	4	1	2	4	1	2	4	1	2	4	1	2
2	4	1	2	4	1	3	4	1	2	4	1	2	4	1	3	4	1	3	4	1	2	4	1
2	4	4	1	2	3	4	4	1	2	3	4	4	1	2	3	4	1	1	2	4	4	1	2

| 1 | 4 | 2 | 2 | 1 | 4 | 4 | 2 | 1 | 4 | 3 | 1 | 1 | 4 | 2 | 2 | 1 | 4 | 4 | 2 | 1 | 4 | 3 | 2 |

8va -

| 1 | 3 | 4 | 1 | 3 | 4 | 1 | 1 | 4 | 2 | 3 | 1 | 1 | 4 | 3 | 2 | 1 | 3 | 2 | 1 | 4 | 4 | 1 | 2 |

8va - - - - - - - - - - - - - - -   *loco*

| 3 | 1 | 2 | 3 | 4 | 1 | 1 | 3 | 2 | 4 | 1 | 1 | 4 | 3 | 1 | 4 | 3 | 1 | 2 | 3 | 4 | 1 | 2 | 4 |

| 4 | 1 | 2 | 2 | 4 | 1 | 1 | 3 | 4 | 1 | 2 | 4 | 4 | 1 | 2 | 2 | 4 | 1 |

2

3

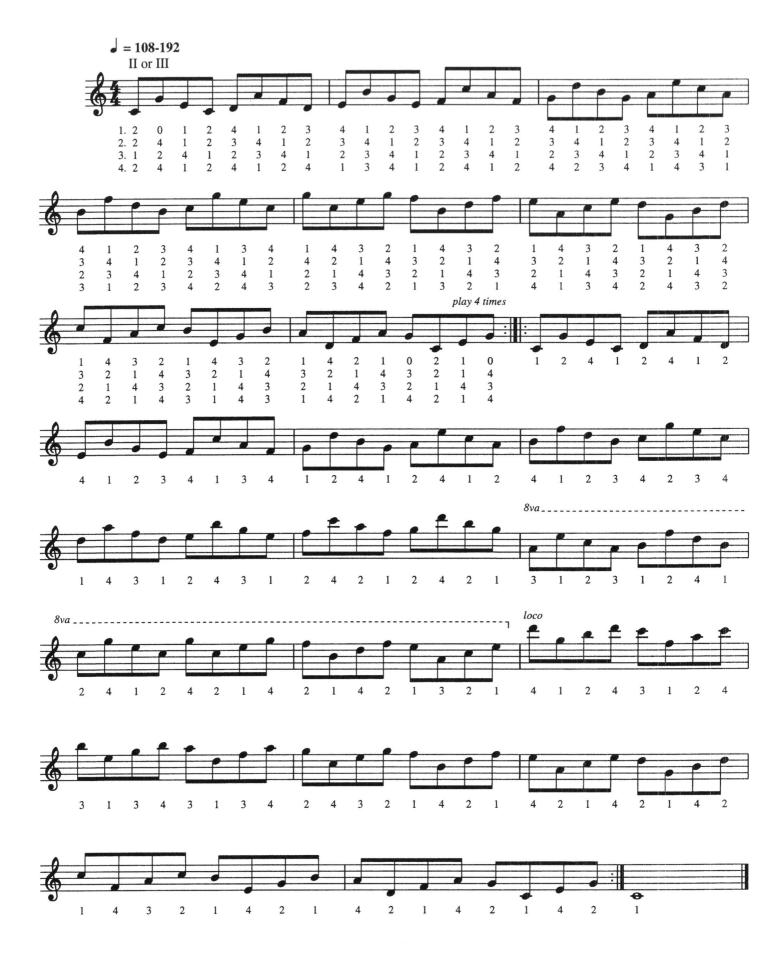

4

5

6

8

9

10

11

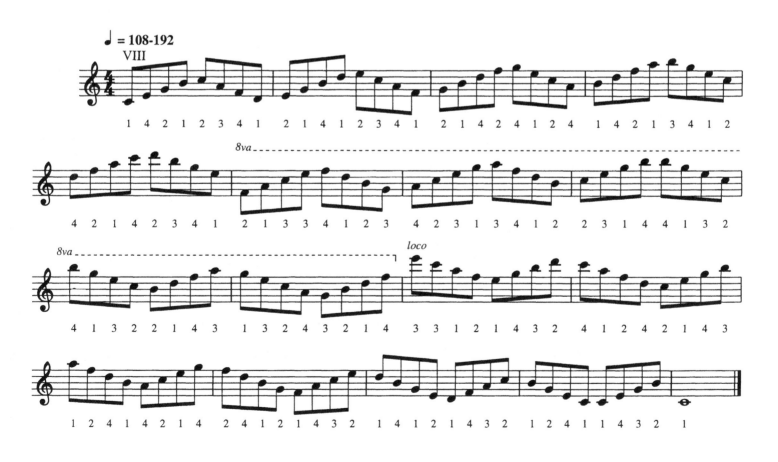

12

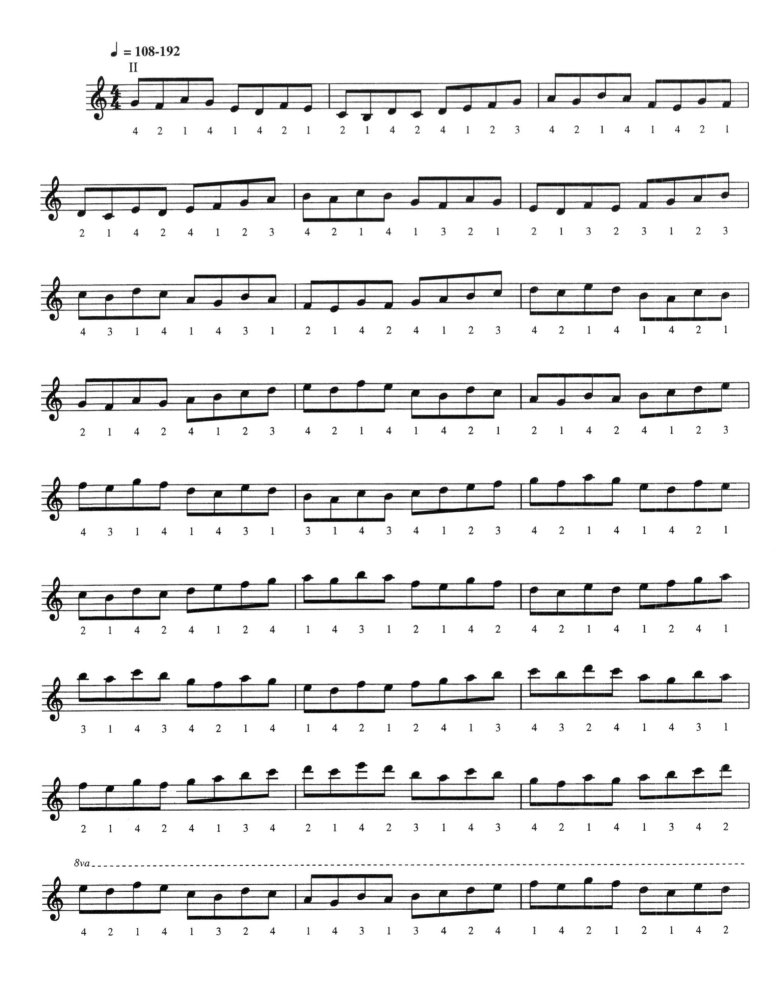

13

14

15

16

17

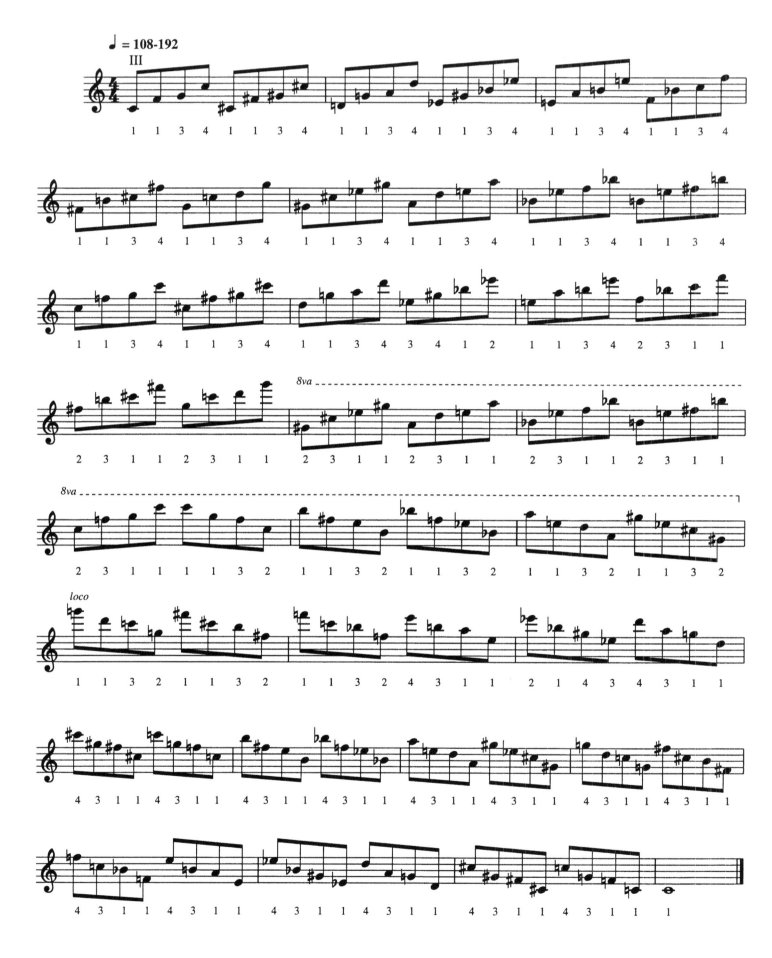

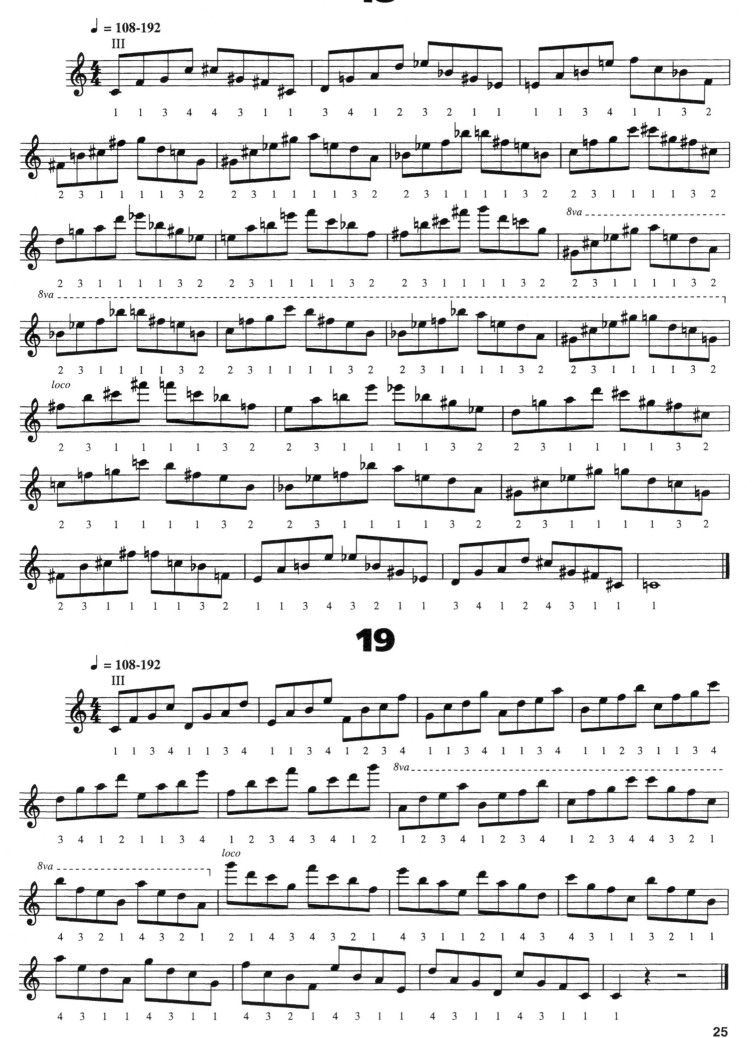

20

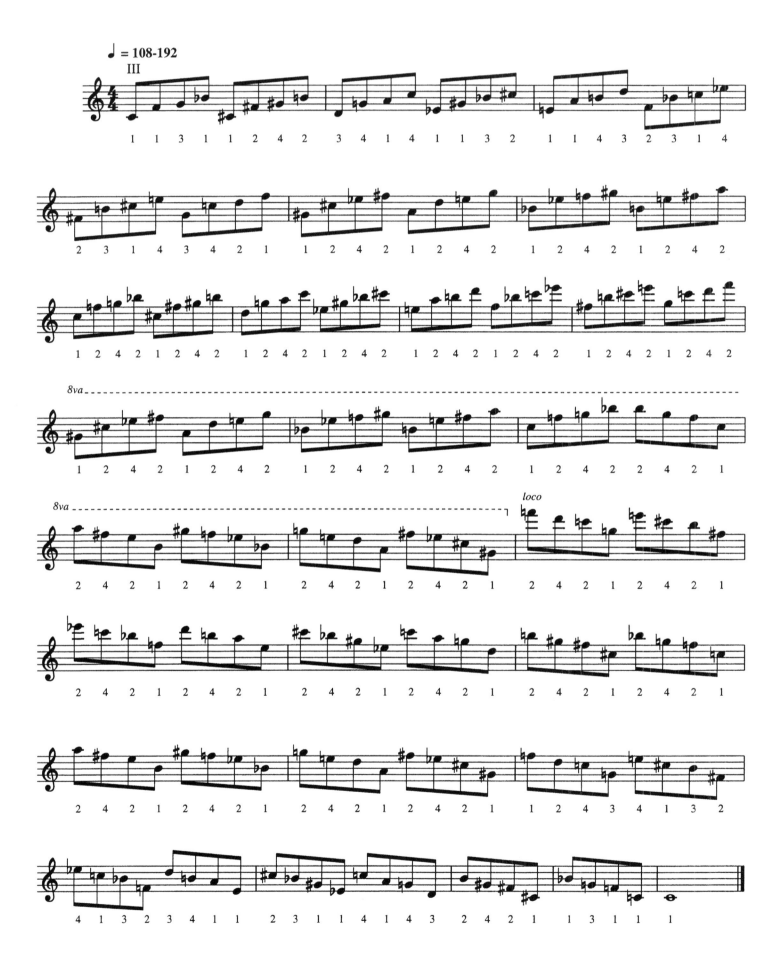

21

22

23

24

25

26

27

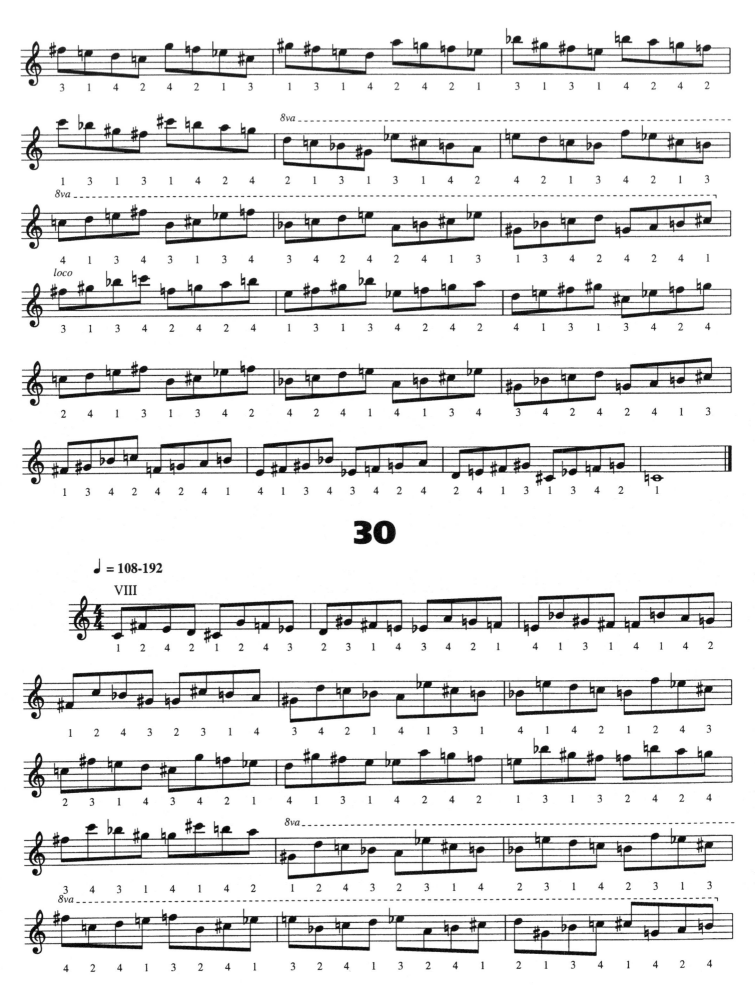

30

31

34

35

36

37

38

39

40

$\quad$ = 108-192

43

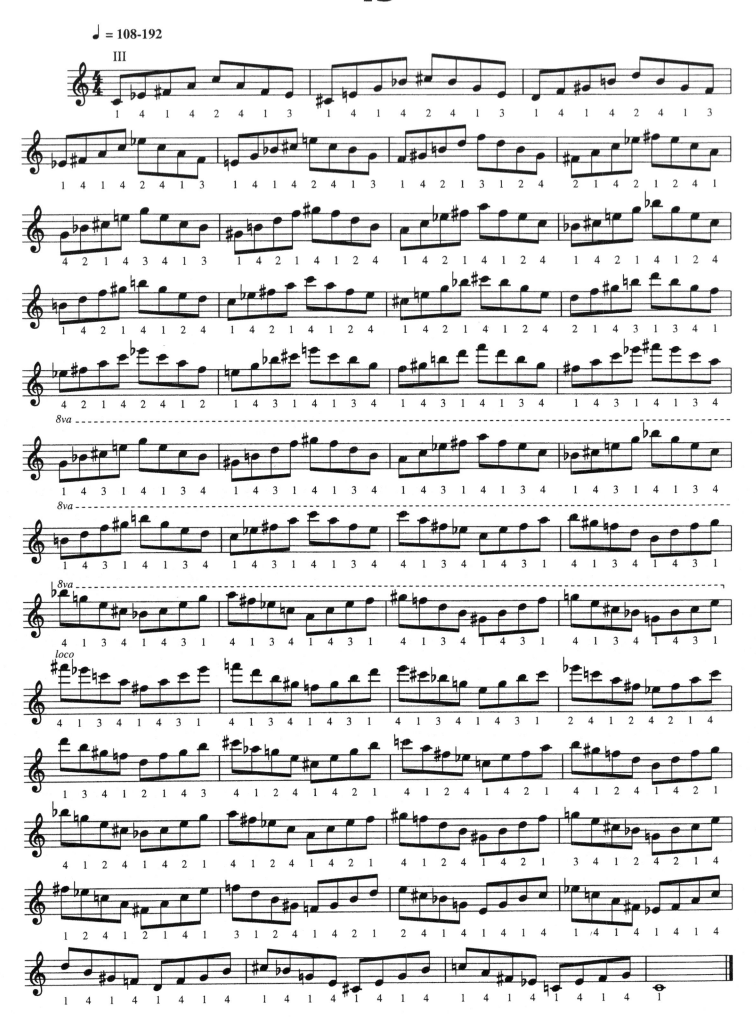

44

45

46

47

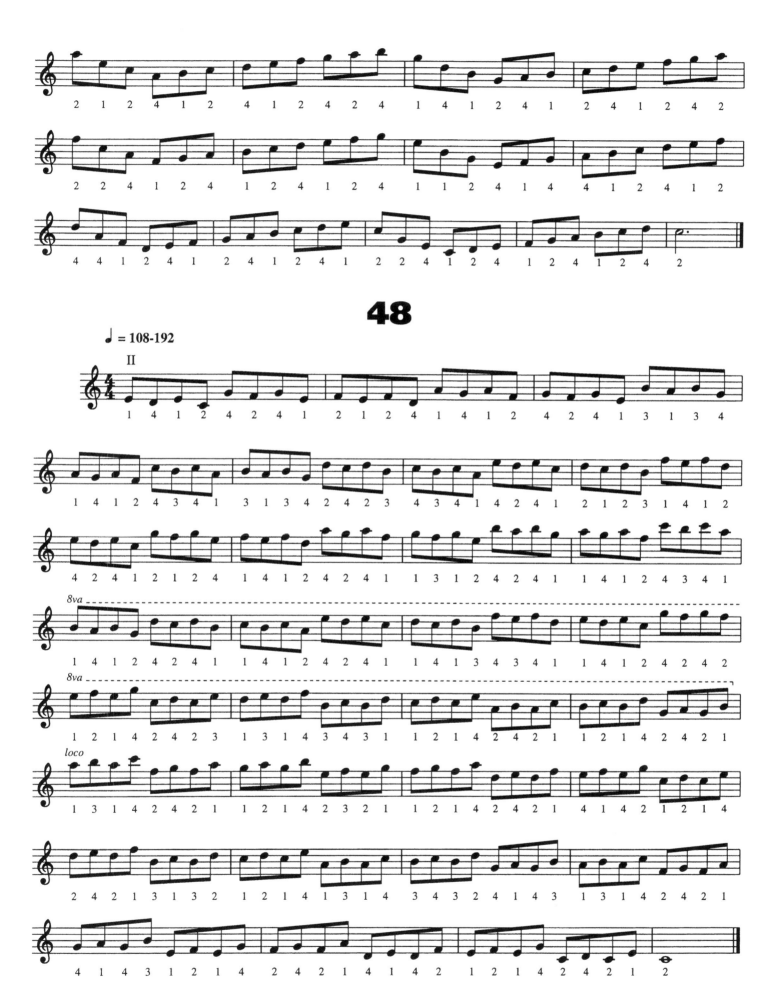

48

49

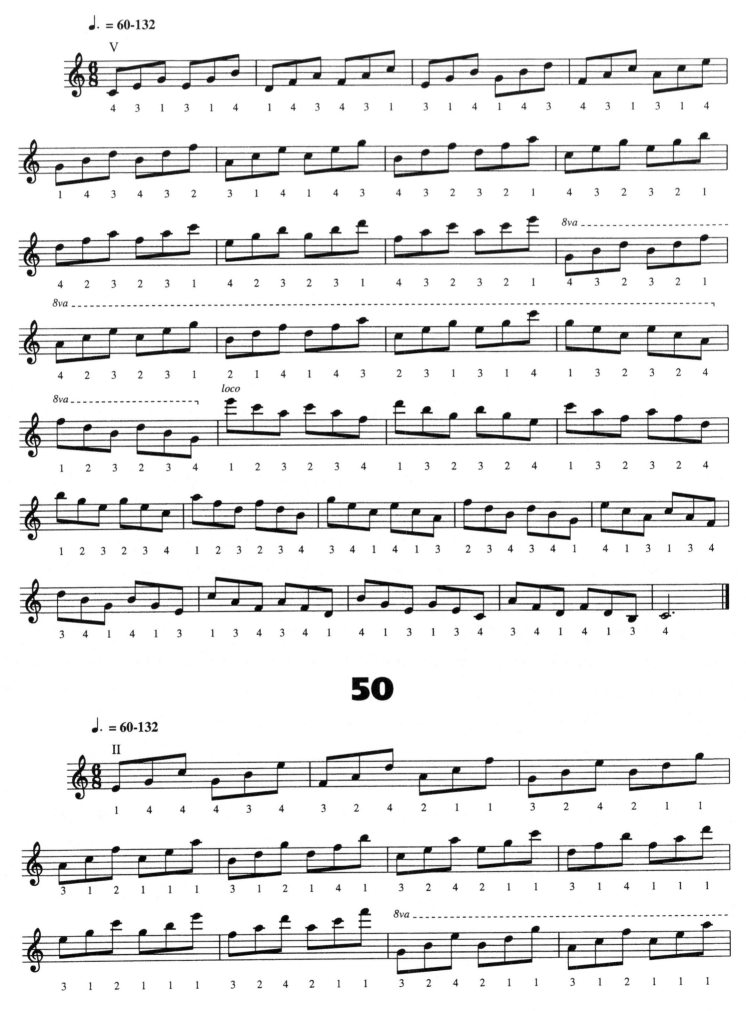

50

51

MUSICIANS INSTITUTE PRESS is the official series of Southern California's renowned music school, Musicians Institute. MI instructors, some of the finest musicians in the world, share their vast knowledge and experience with you – no matter what your current level. For guitar, bass, drums, vocals, and keyboards, MI Press offers the finest music curriculum for higher learning through a variety of series:

ESSENTIAL CONCEPTS	MASTER CLASS	PRIVATE LESSONS
Designed from MI core curriculum programs.	*Designed from MI elective courses.*	*Tackle a variety of topics "one-on one" with MI faculty instructors.*

GUITAR

Acoustic Artistry
by Evan Hirschelman • **Private Lessons**
00695922 Book/Online Audio $19.99

Advanced Scale Concepts & Licks for Guitar
by Jean Marc Belkadi • **Private Lessons**
00695298 Book/CD Pack $19.99

All-in-One Guitar Soloing Course
by Daniel Gilbert & Beth Marlis
00217709 Book/Online Media $29.99

Blues/Rock Soloing for Guitar
by Robert Calva • **Private Lessons**
00695680 Book/CD Pack $19.99

Blues Guitar Soloing
by Keith Wyatt • **Master Class**
00695132 Book/Online Audio $29.99

Blues Rhythm Guitar
by Keith Wyatt • **Master Class**
00695131 Book/Online Audio $19.99

Dean Brown
00696002 DVD $29.95

Chord Progressions for Guitar
by Tom Kolb • **Private Lessons**
00695664 Book/Online Audio $19.99

Chord Tone Soloing
by Barrett Tagliarino • **Private Lessons**
00695855 Book/Online Audio $24.99

Chord-Melody Guitar
by Bruce Buckingham • **Private Lessons**
00695646 Book/Online Audio $19.99

Classical & Fingerstyle Guitar Techniques
by David Oakes • **Master Class**
00695171 Book/Online Audio $19.99

Classical Themes for Electric Guitar
by Jean Marc Belkadi • **Private Lessons**
00695806 Book/CD Pack $15.99

Country Guitar
by Al Bonhomme • **Master Class**
00695661 Book/Online Audio $19.99

Diminished Scale for Guitar
by Jean Marc Belkadi • **Private Lessons**
00695227 Book/CD Pack $14.99

Essential Rhythm Guitar
by Steve Trovato • **Private Lessons**
00695181 Book/CD Pack $16.99

Exotic Scales & Licks for Electric Guitar
by Jean Marc Belkadi • **Private Lessons**
00695860 Book/CD Pack $16.95

Funk Guitar
by Ross Bolton • **Private Lessons**
00695419 Book/CD Pack $15.99

Guitar Basics
by Bruce Buckingham • **Private Lessons**
00695134 Book/Online Audio $17.99

Guitar Fretboard Workbook
by Barrett Tagliarino • **Essential Concepts**
00695712 . . . . $19.99

Guitar Hanon
by Peter Deneff • **Private Lessons**
00695321 . . . . $14.99

Guitar Lick•tionary
by Dave Hill • **Private Lessons**
00695482 Book/CD Pack $21.99

Guitar Soloing
by Dan Gilbert & Beth Marlis • **Essential Concepts**
00695190 Book/CD Pack $22.99

Harmonics
by Jamie Findlay • **Private Lessons**
00695169 Book/CD Pack $13.99

Harmony & Theory
by Keith Wyatt & Carl Schroeder • **Essential Concepts**
00695169 . . . . $22.99

Introduction to Jazz Guitar Soloing
by Joe Elliott • **Master Class**
00695161 Book/Online Audio $19.95

Jazz Guitar Chord System
by Scott Henderson • **Private Lessons**
00695291 . . . . $12.99

Jazz Guitar Improvisation
by Sid Jacobs • **Master Class**
00217711 Book/Online Media $19.99

Jazz, Rock & Funk Guitar
by Dean Brown • **Private Lessons**
00217690 Book/Online Media $19.99

Jazz-Rock Triad Improvising
by Jean Marc Belkadi • **Private Lessons**
00695361 Book/CD Pack $15.99

Latin Guitar
by Bruce Buckingham • **Master Class**
00695379 Book/Online Audio $17.99

Lead Sheet Bible
by Robin Randall & Janice Peterson • **Private Lessons**
00695130 Book/CD Pack $22.99

Liquid Legato
by Allen Hinds • **Private Lessons**
00696656 Book/Online Audio $16.99

Modern Jazz Concepts for Guitar
by Sid Jacobs • **Master Class**
00695711 Book/CD Pack $16.95

Modern Rock Rhythm Guitar
by Danny Gill • **Private Lessons**
00695682 Book/Online Audio $19.99

Modes for Guitar
by Tom Kolb • **Private Lessons**
00695555 Book/Online Audio $18.99

Music Reading for Guitar
by David Oakes • **Essential Concepts**
00695192 . . . . $19.99

The Musician's Guide to Recording Acoustic Guitar
by Dallan Beck • **Master Class**
00695505 Book/CD Pack $13.99

Outside Guitar Licks
by Jean Marc Belkadi • **Private Lessons**
00695697 Book/CD Pack $16.99

Power Plucking
by Dale Turner • **Private Lesson**
00695962 Book/CD Pack $19.95

Progressive Tapping Licks
by Jean Marc Belkadi • **Private Lessons**
00695748 Book/CD Pack $17.99

Rhythm Guitar
by Bruce Buckingham & Eric Paschal • **Essential Concepts**
00695188 Book $19.99
00114559 Book/Online Audio $24.99
00695909 DVD $19.95

Rhythmic Lead Guitar
by Barrett Tagliarino • **Private Lessons**
00110263 Book/Online Audio $19.99

Rock Lead Basics
by Nick Nolan & Danny Gill • **Master Class**
00695144 Book/Online Audio $18.99
00695910 DVD $19.95

Rock Lead Performance
by Nick Nolan & Danny Gill • **Master Class**
00695278 Book/Online Audio $17.99

Rock Lead Techniques
by Nick Nolan & Danny Gill • **Master Class**
00695146 Book/Online Audio $16.99

Shred Guitar
by Greg Harrison • **Master Class**
00695977 Book/CD Pack $19.99

Slap & Pop Technique for Guitar
by Jean Marc Bekaldi • **Private Lessons**
00695645 Book/CD Pack $17.99

Solo Slap Guitar
by Jude Gold • **Master Class**
00139556 Book/Online Video $19.99

Technique Exercises for Guitar
by Jean Marc Belkadi • **Private Lessons**
00695913 Book/CD Pack $15.99

Texas Blues Guitar
by Robert Calva • **Private Lessons**
00695340 Book/Online Audio $17.99

Ultimate Guitar Technique
by Bill LaFleur • **Private Lessons**
00695863 Book/Online Audio $22.99

Prices, contents, and availability subject to change without notice.

7777 W. BLUEMOUND RD. P.O. BOX 13819 MILWAUKEE, WI 53213

www.halleonard.com